The Redneck Guide to Wine Snobbery

By Victor L. Robilio, Jr.

Edited by Thomas B. Storey, Jr.

The Guild Bindery Press
Jackson, Tennessee

and

EFW Commercial Ventures Inc.
Memphis, Tennessee

Published by
EFW Commercial Ventures Inc.
The Guild Bindery Press
Post Office Box 241813
Memphis, Tennessee 38124-1813
telephone (901)685-2078

Printed in the United States of America

5 4 3 2 1

ISBN 1-55793-015-5

Cover design and illustration by Paulette Livers Lambert.

Publication rights: EFW Commercial Ventures Inc.

Table of Contents

Acknowledgments

I wish to thank my spouse Judge Kay Robilio for her enthusiasm and encouragement. Our two daughters, Cecilia Robilio and Catherine Robilio Womack, were also a great source of inspiration to me.

My late father Victor L. Robilio, Sr. (1911-1986) challenged me to spread my knowledge and understanding of wine through a "common sense" wine book. My mother, Cecelia Robertson Robilio, continues to be a model of strength for the entire family.

During the last thirty years I have met many educators, wine industry people, and press personalities. They all furthered my knowledge and encouraged me to learn. Thank you: Robert, Michael, and Tim Mondavi, Dr. Lucio M. Sorre, Charles "Chuck" Mueller, the late Bill Leedom, Gerald Asher, Abdullah Simon, Ruth Ellen Church, Richard Heim, Justine Smith, Nathaniel and Archibald Johnson, Gerry Baggs, the late Charles Quincy, Adam Ballinger, Dr. Richard Vine, Dr. Wayland Tonning, Professor Mary Battle, Helen Karpinski, David Carter, the late Adrian d'Hanis, and Marne Anderson. Special thanks goes to my brother, John R.S. Robilio, for his help with foreign words and phrases. Bill and Connie Burk and Dr. Dan and Stephanie Beasley lent their insights to the book's original outline. Many thanks to Judge Tom Storey of West Point, Mississippi for his proofing and editorial work, and to his wife Sherry for her support. Thanks to Dr. Charles Crawford, head of the Oral History Research Department, Memphis State University, for his time, advice and encouragement. My appreciation also goes to Margo Blake, my loyal, trustworthy, patient secretary who placed this book onto a word processor so that I could complete it. *Tante Grazies!*

Victor L. Robilio, Jr.

Introduction

by Robert Mondavi

No longer the province of East Coast and California gastronomes, good wine is for everyone, including those who call themselves "Rednecks." With *The Redneck Guide to Wine Snobbery*, wine connoisseur and merchant Victor Robilio, Jr. demystifies the cult of the grape for rednecks and rednecks at heart. His nose is in the wineglass, but his tongue is planted firmly in his cheek.

Robilio traces the history of wine and rednecks in American to a common ancestor, Thomas Jefferson. Both a cosmopolitan and an agrarian, Jefferson provides a useful starting point for a witty discussion which makes wine understandable to everyone.

As Victor reminds us, wine is a matter of individual taste and preference, and will reward study and practice—even to the point of snobbery! Not to worry, there's ample room in the book for everyone interested in wine or wanting to be. With Victor's suggestions, culled from over 30 years on the international wine scene, you'll be sure to start off on the right foot. . .and with the right palate.

I've enjoyed Victor's book and I'm sure you will, too. There are not too many "rednecks" in Napa Valley, but y'all come on out for a visit!

Robert Mondavi
Napa Valley
August, 1992

Why a Redneck Guide To Wine?

Quite simply, wine is what Western civilization *is all about*. Think about it, if the whole thing were to fall apart tomorrow, what would be worth saving? When faced with the same question after the break-up of the Roman Empire, Europeans knew the answer. Wine, and maybe democracy, but mainly wine. Granted, this answer may not have been the first one that poured into *your* brain pan, but that only proves how BADLY you need this book. After all, why did you choose this particular wine guide? Was there something about the title that drew you to it? One particular word, perhaps? Was that word *redneck*? If the answer is yes (and you know it is), IT'S O.K. Reputable studies show that most rednecks now own their own satellite dishes and subscribe to at least one magazine other than *Reader's Digest*. More units of information are being fed to the redneck segment of the population than any other. They are poised to peak-out sometime in the early part of the next century. Soon, being a redneck will be chic. So if you're a redneck, SMILE, you are the future: you're going to inherit the earth!

Unfortunately, inheriting the earth also means inheriting the vineyard, and, without the aid of *The Redneck Guide to Wine Snobbery*, that could be catastrophic. Think: what alcoholic beverage is most popularly associated with rednecks? BEER. BEER. BEER. Granted, if life were a TV gameshow like "Family Feud" (the old one with Richard "Newkirk" Dawson), Wild Turkey Bourbon would have made the survey, but BEER would still be THE NUMBER ONE ANSWER. However, it is not the fault of rednecks that they have been relegated to the rear of society's party bus, where only beer and stale Chex mix are served. Rednecks have merely been the victims of **The Great Grape Conspiracy**, a conclave so ultra hush-hush that some readers might think this is all getting a little paranoid.

Not to worry, confusion about wine works the same way as confusion about the stock market and the Electoral College, but not for long. With the publication of the tell-all *Redneck Guide to Wine Snobbery*, **The Great Grape Conspiracy** is reeling from a direct hit at its hip index. The demystification begins now.

Chapter One

A Brief History of Wine

No thing more excellent nor more valuable than wine was ever granted mankind by God.

—*Plato*

And Noah he often said to his wife when he sat down to dine, I don't care where the water goes if it doesn't get into the wine.

—*G.K. Chesterton*

The First Wine Redneck

Although as far as we know he never used the term "redneck," preferring instead the description "yeoman farmer," Thomas Jefferson—Virginian, statesman, architect, writer, planter, scientist, and, yes, **proto-redneck**—was an ardent supporter of the crimson-collared. In fact, in his best-of-all-possible Americas, President Jefferson envisioned a nation of rednecks in the finest, historical sense of the word—fiercely proud and independent farmers whose necks were wrinkled and reddened from honest hard work. Of course, since Jefferson's time rednecks have gotten WAY off track. Factory jobs have led to too much spare time, which in turn led to 4-wheel drive technology, the World Wrestling Federation, Lost Cause-itis, and *Gator Bait II.* Let's just say there is an *unfortunate* side to redneck-ism. But at the same time, let us not be too timid to *wallow* in its more *fortunate* aspects-patriotism, making out in cars, plastic curlers, rockabilly, and the rediscovery of viticulture.

Yes, I said "viticulture, rediscovery of." Did you know that early rednecks like Jefferson drank wine? Did you know that Budweiser *did not even exist* until after World War II? The Jeffersonian philosophy for buying wine was to always "pay a little more, always taste the wine, and always get the best quality." Jefferson's ardent pursuit of quality led him to eventually produce his own grapes. After he and his buddies won the Revolutionary War, Jefferson went to France as American ambassador. His travel throughout France, Germany, and Northern Italy allowed him to obtain many experimental vines and plants and bring them back to his home, Monticello. Unfortunately, unknown mildew and molds destroyed most of Jefferson's vineyards with the exception of the hardy native American grapes, which only produced inferior quality wine. Consequently, **The Great Grape Conspiracy** has labeled Jefferson a failure and will never establish him as the founding father of American wine production. But his sound advice, coupled with his down-to-earth approach to wine, guarantee his position as the primary wine redneck.

California Wines

For our purposes, the history of wine will begin in California in 1769. (Sure, a lot of wine-related stuff happened in Europe and Asia Minor over the preceding two thousand years or so. But that's exactly where **The Great Grape Conspiracy** would like to see this history begin. In fact, unless it's from France, Germany, Spain, or Italy, *avoid* European wine altogether.)

At any rate, while the American colonies were preparing to waylay the British, a young Franciscan padre by the name of Junipera Serra left the Baja peninsula of Mexico. Padre Serra and a ragtag group of Indians and Spanish soldiers trudged northward to San Diego, set up a tiny little mission, and immediately planted some grapevines.

The "mission grapes" were of low quality, but they produced a good crop of basic fruit that yielded dependable table wine. Padre Serra moved up the coast founding many missions, and planting vineyards at every one. Perhaps you've heard of some of them: Los Angeles, Santa Barbara, San Francisco, etc. The missions were generally founded along a highway called "El Camino Real," which, ironically, would later give its name to a classic automobile favored by many rednecks.

Padre Serra established the first winery in California at Mission San Gabriel (inside present day Los Angeles). Sick or weary travelers were always welcomed with a glass of wine and superb food prepared by the kind and hospitable Franciscans.

The Roman Catholic church was running all of the vineyards in California from 1776 to about 1825. At that time, the Europeans arrived on the scene in droves. The first French, Italian, and German immigrants founded their own commercial wineries.

The greatest of all California wine pioneers, however, was Hungarian. "Count" Agoston Haraszthy, a nobleman, was known as the "Father" of nineteenth-century California viticulture. He imported over 100,000 grape vine cuttings of approximately 300 European varieties, and his great enthusiasm resulted in the planting of the new European varieties statewide. Haraszthy was the catalyst for proliferation of the fine wine industry in the state of California.

In the 1860s and 1870s, European vineyards were destroyed by phylloxera, a grapevine root pest. The American vineyards succumbed to phylloxera in the 1880s. We soon discovered, however, that *our native American grapevine roots were phylloxera resistant!* The remaining European and American vineyards were grafted with the native American root stocks for protection. Today, everyone uses the hybrid root stocks to protect their crops from phylloxera.

The California wine industry prospered until 1919 when a curious episode in American history began—the 18th Amendment to the United States Constitution was ratified to prohibit the production, sale, and transportation of alcoholic liquors nationwide. If the truth be told, complacent, teetotalling rednecks allowed the heinous amendment to pass. Anyway, an idea whose time had gone, Prohibition only lasted until 1933, but by that time, many of the fine California vineyards (Beaulieu, Charles Krug, etc.) were reduced to making "table-eating grapes," which have insufficient sugar or acid quantities to make fine wine. A few of the wineries, like Beaulieu, survived Prohibition by selling their wines to various sly religious sects, such as Episcopalians and Catholics, which used sacramental wines.

Soon after the end of Prohibition, the first truly outstanding *Cabernet Sauvignon* made in America was produced in 1936 at

Beaulieu Vineyard by George de Latour. The following year Latour hired Andre Tchelistcheff as his winemaker. Andre, Russian-born, is still alive and is one of the "greatest of the great" winemakers of California. Now retired, Tchelistcheff is revered by all as the "Father" of the modern California Wine Industry.

Robert and Peter Mondavi produced the first California label of Chenin Blanc wine in 1955 at the Charles Krug Winery. Robert Mondavi produced the first California label of Fumé Blanc from sauvignon grapes at his own winery in 1966. The Robert Mondavi Winery continues today as one of the premiere wineries in California and the United States.

Chapter Two

Selection and Enjoyment of Wine

Grudge myself a good wine? As soon as grudge my horse corn.
—William Thackeray

The older woman is like a great wine, she improves with age.
—Anonymous

How to Read a Wine Label

Wine labels are *meant* to intimidate you. It's part of **The Great Grape Conspiracy's** grand design. Why else would they contain so much information (most of it foreign terminology) on such a small surface area?

But never fear, rednecks of the world. All you need to know is that the appropriate bottle label will provide the vintage year, sometimes the bottling date, the brand name, the alcohol strength (usually 10% to 16%), the producer or bottler, and the country and/or state of origin. For example: *Lancers* is the brand name; *Blush* is the type of wine; *Fonseca* is the producer or maker of the wine and *Portugal* is the country of origin. Even long German wine names can be simplified using this foolproof method. Take for example, *Kendermann Veit Piesporter Goldtropchen Spatlese 1986. Kendermann* is the shipper. *Veit* is the small estate producer. *Piesporter* is the village where the grapes were grown. *Goldtropchen* is the vineyard name (which translated means "little gold drops").

In most wine growing regions, the government controls—to some extent—the quality of the grapes and limits the information on the label. After all, sudden wine instability could bring a country's economy crashing to its knees. In France they have *Appellation Controllee,* in the U.S.A. *Wine Agricultural Area,* in Italy *Di Origine Controllata,* and in Germany *Qualitatswein Mit Pradikat.* These agencies control the area in which the grapes are grown and the quantities used in production. They also monitor alcohol content, and, in some cases, the maximum number of grapes that can be produced per acre. Some European governments also can be produced per acre.   Some European governments also regulate the sugar and acid quantities. These controls are stated on the label, and are good indicators of quality, although not infallible.

U.S. Labeling

In the United States the name of the winery (or producer) is usually the most prominent name on the label; for example, Beaulieu, Robert Mondavi, Sterling, Beringer, Kenwood, etc.   Often the grapes may have been grown by the winery, a practice known as "proprietor's growth."

The variety of the grape—Chardonnay, Cabernet Sauvignon, Pinot Noir, etc.—is also   prominent on American labels.   Generic or blended wines omit the use of grape names and instead use names borrowed from France, such as "Burgundy" or "Chablis," or less formally as red or white table wines.

In the United States, the agricultural area is the next most important label designation;   for example,   Napa, Sonoma, Alexander Valley, Stag's Leap, Martha's Vineyard, etc.   These designations may be as broad as "California" or may be as specific as a single vineyard.

French Labeling

Here's where it gets tougher. The evil touch of **The Great Grape Conspiracy** becomes more apparent. For one thing, French labels *almost always* have **French** words on them. The French label emphasizes the agricultural area. This is known as the *Appellation* which again may cite the name of a village—*St. Julien, Margaux, Pauillac*. However, the labels may just contain the name of a single vineyard, as in Burgundy: Corton, Chambertin, Montrachet, Musigny, or just the name of the villege, i.e. Pommard, Volnay, etc.—when the "Appellation Controllee" laws so allow. In Burgundy, the French further complicate matters by combining the names of the most famous vineyards with village names—*Gevrey-Chambertin, Puligny-Montrachet*. In Bordeaux, the vineyards are generally prefixed with the term "Chateau," i.e., Chateau Haut-Brion, Chateau Margaux, Chateaux Lafite-Rothschild, and Chateau Latour. Also in Bordeaux, the wine may be produced and made by the Chateau or vineyard, and thus estate grown, as in "Mis en Bouteilles au Chateau." However, often a Chateau may be purely a "vineyard" whose wine was made elsewhere; there may not even be a house or chateau on the property.

Wines in both Bordeaux and Burgundy may be made by a shipper, or, as the French say, a *negociant*. In Burgundy the name of the shipper is often the most important name to look for on the label. Because there are thousands of independent small plots, or climates, within Burgundy's vineyards, it would be impossible (even for **The Great Grape Conspiracy**) to keep track of the many separate growers by name. Therefore, a reliable shipper's name on a label is often a good indication of quality. Some of the more prominent shippers are Louis Jadot, Louis Latour, Bouchard Pere et Fils, Mommessin, and Barton and Guestier. However, the individual grower's name on the label is also important because one grower's wine may be better than another grower's from the same vineyard, i.e. Domaine de la Romanee-Conti.

Even **The Great Grape Conspiracy** couldn't take the fun out of the next part. In fact, you may even think you already know a little something about vintage. The vintage date on the label indicates in what year the grapes were produced. The actual vintage year is of greater importance in selecting wines from France, Germany, and Italy, less so in California, Oregon, Washington, and Idaho due to the difference in extremes of weather in America.

Vintages, Important or Not

You should make up your own mind about the value of the vintage year on a wine label. You must determine what I call your own "vintage value standard." Mr. Andre Gagey of the French *Louis Jadot* shipping firm, for example, *personally* selects each individual barrel from the farmers that produce his Beaujolais wine. He protects his customers in mediocre years by not buying inferior quality. He has a very high vintage value standard.

Commercial vintage charts should not be readily accepted as legitimate sources of reliable wine standards. Producers of a particular vintage chart are usually very biased. After all, they are part of **The Great Grape Conspiracy** (sounds more like a great name for a psychedelic band every time I say it). They rate some years too low and some too high for purely selfish business reasons. Would you rate a year mediocre if you had invested large amounts of money in wine futures for that year? If you want to rely on a vintage chart, do so as a general reference and only use reputable charts published by unbiased groups such as the International Wine and Food Society (I.W.F.S.).

The prestigious importing company of Austin Nichols was lured into buying large amounts of wine futures for 1972, a mediocre and over-produced vintage year.   In 1973 the inflated price bubble burst.   Austin Nichols lost around $25,000,000 and it took them years to sell their 1972 mediocre wines.   Knowing the widely accepted bad vintage years of important regions—California, Bordeaux, Burgundy—will help you be more selective when buying. Remember, there are always some good wines made in the mediocre vintages.

Follow the advice of proto-redneck Thomas Jefferson.   In writing about his personal wine acquisitions, he states the fact that good firms buy the better wine barrels in off years to protect their valued customers.   He said one should pay a little more for wine during bad years to eliminate the unscrupulous and greedy wine barrel selector.

There are many generic non-vintage wines on the market.   These wines are usually blends (*cuveés* in French) of several grapes which may have been harvested in different years.   Most popular wines are cuveés—screw-cap varieties—Chablis, Burgundy, etc. These are so-called "quaffing" wines.

A generic wine may also be vintage dated and may indeed be an ordinary wine or a very good wine. A satisfactory 1986 or 1987 *Beaulieu* (B.V.) *Chablis* or a great 1984 *Lyeth red* (a premium blend of several Bordeaux varieties) would be two examples.   Both wines are from the northern coast of California.

Vintage Wines Don't Have Screw-Off Caps
Redneck wine snobs demand better quality wine and get it.   The best bet is to visit a wineshop that has only friendly, non-condescending sales personnel. If you happen by accident to enter a store where the people are RUDE, ARROGANT, AND MAKE FREQUENT EXCUSES TO CHECK THEIR STOREROOM, flee the premises at once! You have stumbled into a nest of the **The Great Grape Conspiracy's** agents, obstacles on your road to viticultural bliss.

Except on the low end, price is not always the purest way to identify quality wine, but it's one of the primary criteria. To know whether or not you are in a reputable wine shop, stop and look over the entire store. Are the wines stored lying on their sides or standing upright? If not placed on its side, a bottle of wine will spoil after a few weeks. If the store sells Barbecued Corn Nuts next to their vintage wine section, RUN, DO NOT WALK, out of the store. Your merchant must be knowledgeable and know his stock. Ask him if he tastes his wine regularly. Ask knowledgeable questions to which YOU already know the answers. Ask about the shop's discount policy. A good wine merchant can be your best friend; a bad or ignorant one, an insidious enemy.

Proper Restaurant Decorum

As for selecting and enjoying wine (without embarrassing yourself) at a restaurant, here are a few guidelines:

1. If the establishment has a *sommelier* (wine waiter) or a knowledgeable maitre'd, listen and consider his recommendation. Old bottles need to be aired out. Open them about 30 minutes prior to tasting them.

2. The kind of wine depends entirely on the food being served. Do not prematurely select the wine. Wait until every guest has ordered so that you may choose the best wine to complement the entrees. More than one choice may be needed if, for example, some have ordered fish while others have ordered steak.

3. A full bottle serves about 4 to 6 persons. You may need a second bottle if more than that are present at the table. Of course, if you want to get really plowed, one bottle = one person is a quick and easy formula to remember. (But seriously, don't drive home or operate heavy equipment should you feel drunk.)

4. The wine will be offered to you first. After all, you are the redneck wine snob. Examine the cork, but do not sniff it. If it is not firm or full or intact, the wine may be spoiled. Next, the waiter should offer you a small amount in your glass. Swirl it and make sure the nose is typical and does not smell of cork. Next, taste a small amount. If it passes, gesture to the waiter. A nod is most acceptable, but a wink could be fun too.

5. Unless the waiter is very experienced, ask him to leave the full bottle next to you. Otherwise, instruct the waiter to check with

you before pouring more because many restaurants threaten their waiters with physical violence if they fail to "keep the glasses full." The result is *wasted wine* and *money*, and high morale among the wait staff. Sometimes the meal goes so well that another bottle is appropriate, so order it. Any wine left in the bottle belongs to you. Don't be ashamed to brown bag it and take it home (Unless, of course, local ordinances prevent it).

6. In a restaurant, the trick is to buy only medium to lower priced wines, looking for the best valued wine that complements your meal. After a while, you will be able to remember the store prices and compare them to the menu prices. Reasonably priced restaurant wine is never more than double the retail price.

7. If any bottle of wine tastes like vinegar, it is BAD. Send it back. Don't make a big production over it (unless you've got an angle on benefitting off the restaurant's mistake by getting a free meal). This seldom occurs. In my thirty years of tasting, I have only sent back six bottles.

8. Between courses, sherbet, such as lemon or raspberry, is often served to cleanse the palate. Do not request special flavors like "Rocky Road."

NOTE: To acquire wine recall knowledge, it is a good idea to taste a little of many different wines. I like to try half glasses or quarter glasses in wine and food bars. There are many places to do just this; New Orleans is home to Flagon's Wine Bar on Magazine Street and Memphis boasts Le Chardonnay on Madison Avenue.

Wine Tasting: Just Follow Your Tongue

Tasting techniques are easily learned and easily recalled. The tip of your tongue signals you as to whether the wine is sweet or dry. The sides of your tongue up front give you the density of fruit acidity found in the wine. (Compare the fruit acidity in white wine to a glass of fresh orange juice, which contains about one half percent natural alcohol.)

The roof of your mouth and the sides of your tongue in the rear of your mouth relay the amount of tannic acid (*tannin*) found in red wines. This is called *pucker power* because beverage bitters produce this same sensation as do high tannic red wines. Tannin dissipates as fine red wines mature with age.

Aroma denotes the smell of the grape variety or varieties used. The *bouquet* usually refers to the complexity that the grape has derived from the blending, aging, and other methods of the wine maker.

Your nose can identify more than 300 different odors. Hold a small amount of wine in your mouth and cup your tongue. Inhale through your mouth, then exhale through your nose. Your olfactory nerve will compute the wine's exact flavor bouquet instantly, not to mention the fact that the noise created by inhaling and exhaling will make you *sound* like a professional wine taster.

When you finally swallow, let the wine flow over the entire roof of your mouth to experience the full sensation and taste. If the wine flavor continues to linger in your mouth after swallowing, the wine is said to have a long "aftertaste" and if pleasant, indicates high quality. Close your eyes and concentrate on each wine's smell (aroma and bouquet) and distinct taste. Block out all other thoughts and you will become an excellent taster. Keep notes in a small spiral notebook for future references.

Chapter Three

Harmony of Food and Grape

That they the hearts from out the breasts may tear,
Cut off their heads then drag them by the hair
And cast them on the dunghill of the swine,
That sows and porkers on their flesh may fare,
The vintners that put water in our wine.

—*Francois Villan*

A meal without wine is like a day without sunshine.
—*Anthelme Brillat-Savarin*

What is the best wine for a given meal? All I can hope to do is give you some general guidelines. If you want cold Cabernet Sauvignon with warm barbecued chicken, then so be it. You can rest assured, however, that if you pull a stunt like that in public, there will be agents of the highly mysterious and paranoid **Great Grape Conspiracy** on hand to make you FEEL your mistake. The following rudimentary suggestions will help familiarize the aspiring redneck wine snob with the basic rules of selection. The goal, of course, is to modify and, ultimately, transcend these rules with one's own creativity.

•Heavier food calls for full bodied, more robust, and pungent wines. Lighter-bodied, still, and sparkling wines complement lighter, more delicate foods. (Isn't this easy?)

•Serving red wines with red meat and white with white meat is a good rule, but one meant to be broken. Many white meats go well with a light, fruity red wine. A nice medium bodied Pinot Noir or Beaune from Burgundy will go nicely with your holiday turkey and all its trimmings. A nice Riesling or medium bodied Chardonnay would be equally suitable. Depending on the sauce or garnish, veal is usually served with Pinot Noir or Red Burgundy, but a Chardonnay and White Burgundy may also be appropriate. Pork is adaptable to either red or white wine depending on the sauces used and how the meat is cooked.

•Most fish entrees require white wine, but a nicely baked spicy seafood dish is sometimes best offset with a red! Experiment! Enjoy!

•Pay attention to seasonings.

•Here in the South, where outdoor grilling is very popular, try a rich California Red Zinfandel with basted spare ribs. California Fumé Blanc (or Sauvignon Blanc) goes well with grilled chops or tenderloin of pork roast.

Cooking With Wine

Most great chefs cook with wine. Wine adds character and flavor to many foods, especially when blended in sauces and gravy.

A good rule to follow is to use the same type of grape as will be in the wine you choose to serve with the dish. You don't have to use the same wine! Only a wine snob flunky of **The Great Grape Conspiracy** (not a redneck snob like you) would use a $25.00 bottle of reserve Cabernet Sauvignon to cook with! Instead, use a much less expensive everyday California Cab and serve the expensive reserve Cabernet with it. When
you cook with wine, remember the boiling removes the alcohol so only flavor is left!

Some home recipes that have been used with success follow. Try them, and, in true redneck spirit, modify them to your taste!

The Editor's Mushroom and Red Wine Sauce

(For beef steaks or rare roast beef for 4)
1   Clove of fresh shallots (green onions or vidalia may be
        substituted [1/4 c])
8-10 Spanish olives, diced
1/4c   Red wine (California or French Cabernet, Merlot, or
Pinot Noir)
1   4oz. 402 can mushroom buttons, partially drained (can
substitute or add sliced)
        OR
16-20 Fresh mushrooms (halved large ones)
1T   Dale's Steak Sauce or soy sauce based substitutes
1/3   Stick of butter or butter substitute

To taste   Lemon Pepper—we prefer Lawry's (for low salt, try Lawry's Salt Free No. 17 Seasoning)
2T   Olive oil
1T   Cornstarch

1. Saute shallots or onions in skillet in olive oil over medium heat.
2. Add mushrooms and olives.
3. Add 1/2 of wine, reserve the rest.
4. Bring to a slow boil.
5. Add seasonings and butter.
6. Once a slow boil returns, stir cornstarch into wine reserve to dissolve, and pour into skillet to thicken.
7. Bring back to a low boil, then cover skillet and turn off the heat.
8. Ready to serve (sauce will stay hot while you barbeque your steaks).

Southern Lamb Chops and Pinot Noir

2   1 to 1-1/2 inch thick lamb chops
2T   oregano
1/8 to 1/4c   Pinot Noir

Pat oregano on both sides of chops, wrap in plastic wrap and refrigerate for a couple of hours. Pepper with fresh ground pepper and drizzle a small amount of olive oil. Pan broil 7 minutes on each side, drizzle with Pinot Noir after broiling and enjoy. Serve with a fine California Pinot Noir or French Red Burgundy from the Côte de Beaune.

Mississippi Chili and Red Wine*
(*a good inexpensive California Cabernet Sauvignon is best)

Cook 6 slices of bacon, cut in thick pieces, until done but limp. Saute a large purple onion. Add 1 lb. ground round and 1 lb. low fat sausage. Stir fry till done.

ADD
1/2c Worstershire sauce
1c red wine
2 cans tomatoes
1 can Rotel tomatoes
2T Chili powder (or more to taste)

Simmer for an hour; add 3 cans beans—kidney, red beans, garbanzo or one of each. Simmer another 30 minutes

Beef Liver Zinfandel

Thinly sliced liver—veal liver is best but calves liver is fine. Dredge in flour, lemon pepper and oregano mixture; pan fry in olive oil; pour small amount (2 to 3 oz) Zinfandel over liver as cooking is completed. Serve with a full-bodied California Red Zinfandel.

Sherry's Veal Scallopini

6   slices of veal
4   green onions
8oz   fresh mushrooms
Lemon pepper
Chardonnay (about 2 to 3 oz.)
Olive oil

Dredge veal in flour and sprinkle with lemon pepper. Saute green onions; add a small amount of olive oil, sliced mushrooms and cook for a few minutes. Move over to one side of skillet. Adding small amounts of olive oil, quickly pan-fry veal. Add about 1/3c wine to veal drippings to make a sauce. Pull mushrooms and onions back over veal slices. You may have to add a little more wine.

Chapter Four

Storage and Service of Wine

Oh, for a draught of vintage that hath been
Cool'd a long age in the deep delved earth,
Tasting of flora and the country green,
Dance and provencal song and sunburnt mirth.

—*John Keats*
I'd rather have a bottle in front of me than a frontal lobotomy.
—*Walter P. Armstrong, Jr.*

Not in the Barn, Unless it's Climate Controlled

As wine is a perishable food product, don't store yours in the kitchen or any room where the heat is above 65° F. Wine ages quickly in such environments and the cooking process is induced by 75° to 80° F temperatures. Store wine in a dark, cool and semi-humid room or basement. Preferably, the bottles should be placed on their sides in a stable closet or location where the temperature is maintained between 55° and 57° F.

The rest of this chapter is incredibly SPECIFIC, so get ready for some real nuts and bolts info. Sometimes you will need to chill reds at least 12° to 15° F below room temperature. This is especially true with French Burgundies and Beaujolais, American Zinfandel, Gamay, and Pinot Noir. Fuller bodied red wines such as Cabernet Sauvignon and Bordeaux are best when served between 60° and 65° F. To the contrary do not serve your wines too cold or they will be "iced" out and tasteless. Room temperature is a good rule of thumb, unless your room is 80° Fahrenheit!

Premium white wines are usually served between 40° and 55° F; lesser wines colder 35° to 45°F. As a general rule, remember that the better the white wine (except dessert wines), the higher the serving temperature. Rich, full bodied California Reserve Chardonnays and vineyard Burgundies of· France require only moderate chilling! All dessert wines: Sauternes, Late Harvest Johannisberg Riesling, German ice-wines, Spatlese, Auslese, Beerenauslese, and Trockenbeeren Auslese should be served well-chilled—at approximately 40° F.

Serving wine at home can be more or less elegant than being served at a restaurant, depending on the occasion. As in a restaurant, use a clear, 6, 8 or 10 ounce goblet or fluted wine glass (preferably the goblet).   If more than one wine is to be served, then the glass to be used first is always the one on the inside. Again, fill only 1/3 to 1/2 of the glass, depending on its size (1/2 for 6-8 oz., 1/3 for larger).

As host, you should pour a small amount in your glass to check the aroma and taste before serving your guests.

White and sparkling wine should be cooled to about 45° F in ice and water; after serving, the remaining wine may be returned to the ice bucket to stay cool for the second serving. Watch your guests' glasses during the dinner and offer more when the glass is empty or almost empty. If you are serving more than one wine or more than one food course, it is best to have separate glasses for each course.

A popular misconception is that red wine usually requires either decanting or breathing. Only certain red wines benefit from these practices, though. Old, heavy bodied wine from Bordeaux and very old Cabernet Sauvignon from California must be decanted, or else the sediment thrown off will make every glass bitter.   You can see sediment by looking through the bottle in front of a bright light, especially a candle. Decant your wine by holding the bottle horizontally. The top should be slightly higher than the decanter. Gently pour the wine into the decanter while holding the neck over a candle or a light bulb. When you begin to see solid particles in the neck, stop. Serve the wine from the decanter, but always place the empty bottle on the table or within your guests' view so they can see what they are drinking.

Toasts

Toasts provide an easy vehicle for shows of affection, humor, friendship, and love; stupidity can easily gloss all these sentiments should too much wine be mixed with words. I have included some of my favorite toasts so that you may enlarge your repertoire.

May friendship, like wine, improve as time advances.
—an old English quote

May you be as prolific as your guests are verbose.
—a wedding reception favorite

Should you be 'Blowin in the Wind,' may you not hit any chimes.
—Bob Dylan

I would rather God took my life than ask my son-in-law for clothes.
—old Kurdish toast

Your top to my top, your bottom to my bottom, your middle to my middle. It is because I like you a lot that I will give you a little.
—Anonymous

Many's a slip between the wine cup and the lip.
—Anonymous

May you live to be 100 years old and I am the last person to see you before you kick off.
—Anonymous

Chapter Five

Great Wines of the World

God loves fermentation just as dearly as he loves vegetation.
—*Ralph Waldo Emerson*

France

Beaune, France is the capital of the Burgundy wine trade. It is also the location of the famous Hotel Dieu, commonly called *Hospices de Beaune*. Each fall, after the vintage, wine brokers from around the world come to the *Hospices de Beaune* for a world famous wine auction. The prices fetched for various Chardonnay and Pinot Noir casks determine the value of the current vintage harvest. Beaune is thus mecca for wine enthusiasts.

In France the two prominent varieties of red grapes are the *Cabernet Sauvignon* of Bordeaux and the *Pinot Noir* grapes from Burgundy and Champagne. The Cabernet Sauvignon is the principal grape of one of the most famous vineyards in Bordeaux, Chateau Mouton Rothschild. The Pinor Noir grape rivals the Cabernet Sauvignon as the greatest red grape of France. It is used for both Champagne and the great red Burgundy of France. One of the most famous red Burgundies is the great vineyard, Chambertin.

There is only one prominent white grape in France, the Chardonnay. It produces the world famous Champagne as well as the great French white Burgundies. *Le Montrachet* is universally recognized as the most famous Chardonnay vineyard in the Burgundy wine district.

The second most prominent French white grape is the Sauvignon Blanc. It produces the Pouilly Fumé and Sancerre wines of the Loire River Valley. When properly made, this grape produces a very smooth, crisp, dry, and flinty (rocky) tasting dinner wine. Sancerre, from the Loire Valley, was a favorite of the late, great writer Ernest Hemingway (1899-1961). La Doucette Pouilly Fumé is the best known of the many great Sauvignon Blanc wines produced in the Loire Valley of France.

Besides price, how do we generally rank wines? The French have adopted both official and unofficial classification systems. The most famous official classification system was developed in 1855 for the Medoc region of Bordeaux. Approximately 62 wines were classified into five separate groups known as *Premier Crus* (First growths), and *Second, Third, Fourth, and Fifth* growths. There is very little quality difference from one growth to another.

This system has withstood the passage of time rather well. However, the system should be updated to include deserving newer wines and exclude some of the older ones which no longer meet the standards. Some third growths are now sometimes better than some seconds. However, when a bordeaux label has an 1855 classification, or "Cru Classe 1855" or other words to that effect, you have good reason to expect that the bottle contains historical wine that should be of very good to exceptional quality (and pay a higher price accordingly).   There are also many fine unclassified Bordeaux known as "Cru Bourgeois" which are fine bargains when carefully selected. Ch. Coufran Haut (Medoc), Ch. De Marbuzet (Saint Estephe), and Ch. Gloria (St. Julien) are three you might try.

In the Burgundy region, the upper echelon wines are also classified. Some thirty-one vineyards in the hills of Côte d'Or (including Côte de Beaune and Côte de Nuits) are classified as *Grand Crus*, and thus form the upper crust of French Burgundy. Some of the most famous and rare of these wines include *Chambertin Clos de Beze, Musigny, Clos de Tart, Clos Vougeot, Montrachet, Corton, Corton Charlemagne,* and *La Romanee-Conti*. Somewhat confusing is the second level of great Burgundies—*Premier Grand Crus*—of which there are many; most are very fine, expensive wines.   The confusing part is the use of premier for the second level of quality; the term is also used in Bordeaux for the first level. Burgundy rarely identifies the classification on the label, since only the Grand Crus may use the name of the vineyard on the label without any other designation.

Similar labeling practices are followed in Chablis and Beaujolais; there are nine Grand Crus in Beaujolais and seven Grand Crus in Chablis.   There are numerous Premier Crus in Chablis, all of good to excellent quality.   The Grand Crus of Beaujolais are Morgan,

Chiroubles, Chenas, Fleurie, Regnie (new kid on the block), Brouilly, Côte de Brouilly, St. Amour, and Moulin-A-Vent. The second level of Beaujolais, labeled *Beaujolais-Villages*, are from a group of approximately 32 villages. All other Beaujolais wines are entitled to be labeled *Beaujolais*. The primary red grape of Beaujolais, unlike the rest of Burgundy, is *Gamay*.

In Chablis, there are seven Grand Crus of the rich steely, dry Chardonnay: Bougros, Les Preuses, Vaudesir, Grenouilles, Valmur, Les Closiand (another new kid on the block), and Moutonne. Chablis Premier Crus are very fine wines, many of them just use "Premier Cru" on the label with the name of the vineyard often being omitted. Other lesser known Chablis are known as just *Chablis*.

Germany

The most famous German grape is the white *Riesling*. This grape is also known as the Johannisberg Riesling. Not all Riesling grapes are grown in Germany, however. True Riesling grapes are exquisite; they blend a remarkable combination of fruity and acidic flavors. Late harvest Riesling grapes need a long growing season so they cannot be harvested every year. Consequently, late harvest Riesling grapes only make up a small portion of Germany's annual grape harvest.

U.S.A.

As a varietal, the red Pinot Noir grape is now achieving great things in the United States, especially in Oregon and the cooler regions of the northern coast of California. California and Washington state also produce many great Cabernet Sauvignon wines. Their quality is without parallel in both North and South America. The following wines are considered among the top American Cabernet Sauvignons: Beaulieu Vineyard Georges de Latour Private Reserve, Heitz Wine Cellars Martha's Vineyard, Robert Mondavi Reserve, Beringer Private Reserve, Charles Krug Vintage Selection, Opus One, Lyeth Red, Kenwood Artist Label & Jack London, and Columbia Red Willow (Washington State). Both the Lyeth and Opus One blend Cabernet Sauvignon and other Bordeaux style grapes (Merlot, Malbec, Petit Verdot, and Cabernet Franc). To be labeled as Cabernet Sauvignon, the listed wines may use some of the other grapes, but must contain at least 75% Cabernet Sauvignon.

California produces a great many top quality white Chardonnay grape wines. We suggest the following for their consistent high quality: Robert Mondavi Reserve, Beaulieu Los Carneros, Beringer Private Reserve, Sequoia Grove Carneros, Meridian Chardonnay *Edna Valley*, and Montecello Cellars Chardonnay *Corley Reserve*.

Many white Johannisberg Riesling grapes are produced in California and Washington state. Some of the best producers are Firestone, Beringer, Beaulieu, Robert Mondavi, Hogue, and Columbia. We prefer the drier styles and hope the American wineries will make crisp, dry and flinty Rieslings like our friends in Alsace, France.

Varietal Wines

Varietal wines are named after a particular grape variety. Example: Cabernet Sauvignon is a grape variety. If it is produced in the United States, the B.A.T.F. (Beer, Alcohol, Tobacco, and Firearms) rule requires that every bottle labeled as Cabernet Sauvignon contain 75% of pure Cabernet Sauvignon. Most major premium red wine producers give 85%-100% Cabernet Sauvignon per bottle. Chardonnays are almost always 100% Chardonnay.

In the United States, generic wines have appropriated the names of old world geographical areas: Chablis, Burgundy, and Chianti. These terms were used by immigrants from those areas who borrowed the misleading, inaccurate names as a sales tool.

The word *blend* or *cuveé*, a French term which denotes a special label, gives the wine-maker lots of latitude in producing a wine. The wine-maker can use several grape varieties to produce the blend. I don't like to buy a bottle unless the grape varieties are listed on the label. These blends can be, and often are, table wines of average quality. Some table wines may be extraordinary classic wines of great virtue such as Lyeth Red, Opus One, and Sterling Private Reserve. These super premium blends from similar Bordeaux grapes are often called *Meritage* or simply Red Table Wine, containing blends of the Bordeaux varietals, i.e. Cabernet Sauvignon, Merlot, Petit Verdot, Cabernet Franc, and Malbec. Again, price is usually the great separator of ordinary and classic premium wines.

Chapter Six

The Principal Wine Grapes and Regions

Wine is light, held together by water.

—Galileo

Wine is just an opinion.

—Victor L. Robilio, Sr.

Okay, basically, you've got TWO THINGS to remember. On the one hand you've got your PRINCIPAL GRAPES--Chardonnay, Cabernet Sauvignon, Pinot Noir, etc. Collectively, they are known as *Vinifera* (originally native grapes of ancient Europe). While on the other hand, wine regions are historically designated by geographic names--Bordeaux, Burgundy, Chablis, Napa, Sonoma, etc. It is important to realize that there is crossover between these two identification methods. For example, although the grape name never appears on the label, the French Red Burgundy is made strictly from Pinot Noir grapes. In California, where the Chardonnay grapes are harvested from different agricultural areas— Napa and Sonoma Valley—the label emphasis, however, remains on "Chardonnay."

The guide below will show how grape varietals from Vinifera grapes relate to principal wine regions. Certain wine and food recommendations will also be made. Master this list and it will be like having a BLACK BELT in KARATE!

Riesling (Johannisberg Riesling)
(Rees'ling) light white wine. (In the United States it is sometimes known as white Riesling).

ORIGIN: Germany
RECOMMENDED COUNTRIES: Germany, US, France (only in Alsace) Australia, Yugoslavia, Balkans, Austria, Hungary.
TASTE: Dry (less than 2% sugar) to sweet (more than 17% sugar). Taste becomes drier with age.

COLOR: When youthful, pale green. Hue turns golden as the wine ages.
SMELL (AROMA AND BOUQUET): When young, intensely fresh and fruity. When mature, flowery and fragrant.
HOW TO SERVE: Serve dry Riesling (less than 2% sugar) 45° to 55° F with lighter dishes, deep sea and fresh water fish, chicken, turkey, and lighter meats. Serve sweet Riesling (more than 3% sugar) chilled with unsalted crackers, fruit and cheese, or sweet desserts.
PRICE RANGE: $4.00 to $40.00
BEST BUYS: $6.00 to $12.00
IMPORTANT ORIGIN FACTS:
In 1775, the Benedictine monastery of St. John the Baptist, near Rudesheim, developed the Riesling grape. This grape produces the great white wines from the Mosel and Rhine River Valleys in Germany and is prominent in eastern Europe. One California favorite of ours is the Firestone Johannisberg Riesling from Brooks and Kate Firestone.

Gewürztraminer
(Guh-vurts-tra-mee-ner) mid to heavy-bodied white wine
ORIGIN: Alsace, France
RECOMMENDED BEST COUNTRIES: US, France (only in Alsace).
TASTE: Dry (.25% residual sugar) to semi-dry (2.5% residual sugar).
COLOR: Water white when young. Golden straw when aged.
SMELL (AROMA AND BOUQUET): Fragrant, intense, and lingering.
HOW TO SERVE: Dry Gewürztraminer, less than 1% sugar, is a complement to monkfish, scallops, trout, most any pork dish, including Southern-style barbecue ribs and shoulders. Serve sweet Gewürztraminer with fresh fruit, mild to medium cheeses or as a dessert. Also goes well with candied baked ham.
PRICE RANGE: $6.99 to $9.99
BEST BUY : $7.99
IMPORTANT ORIGIN FACTS: The grape was brought to Alsace by the Romans. Originally, it came from the Tyrol Mountains of northern Italy. It has been cultivated throughout history and has improved greatly in quality. During the German military occupations of Alsace from 1871-1918, and again from 1940-1944, the quality of Gewurztraminer production suffered greatly. Today, the quality is very high, and US brands are becoming drier

and fuller in taste, much like the Alsation originals. We especially enjoy the *Dopff Au Moulin* from Alsace.

Semillon

(Say-mee-yohng) medium to lighter white wine
ORIGIN: France
RECOMMENDED COUNTRIES: US, France, Australia, Israel, and Chile
TASTE: Usually dry (.25% residual sugar) to semi-dry (1.5%)
COLOR: Pale water white when young. Light golden when aged.
SMELL (AROMA AND BOUQUET): Herbaceous, lemony, flowery, clean and crisp, fleeting grassy scent.
HOW TO SERVE: Chilled slightly with lighter picnic dishes. Goes well with chicken, fresh and salt water fish, ham, and most salads.
PRICE RANGE: $4.00 to $10.00
BEST BUY : $8.00
IMPORTANT ORIGIN FACTS: The Semillon grape is blended with the Sauvignon Blanc grape to produce the sweet and luscious Sauternes and Barsac great dessert wines of Bordeaux France. The Semillon and the Sauvignon Blanc are also blended to produce the wonderfully light, dry, and crisp Graves wines of France. Wineries such as Lyeth and Vichon are now blending the two grapes in the North Coast of California and produce a Graves-styled dinner wine. Semillon is very flexible and complements fish and most white meat dishes.

We recently tasted some Tyrrells Semillon from South Australia. It had freshness and delicacy that is difficult to find in a non-blended Semillon. Always try to buy dry Semillon with a recent vintage date. However, the blended dessert wines are often very long-lived! (*See* Sauvignon Blanc, also.)

Sauvignon Blanc

(So-vee-yohng-blawnk) medium to heavy bodied white wine
ORIGIN: France
RECOMMENDED COUNTRIES: US, France, Australia, Chile, Israel
TASTE: Usually dry (.25% residual sugar) to semi-dry (1.5%)
COLOR: Pale water white when young. Golden straw when aged.

SMELL (AROMA AND BOUQUET): Metallic, crisp, clean, mountain fresh, flinty, rocky, herbaceous, gravelly, delicate, artichoke aroma
HOW TO SERVE: Chilled or at cellar temperature of 60° F. Open 15 minutes before serving to expand wine's complexity. Delicate bouquet will develop even more when oxygen mixes with it in your glass. Serve with pompano, lobster, oysters, crab meat, ham or tuna salads, chicken, trout and frog legs. Especially good with lighter meat and pork dishes when they are grilled over an open fire.
PRICE RANGE: $5.00 to $22.00
BEST BUY : $9.00
IMPORTANT ORIGIN FACTS: Originally, the Sauvignon Blanc was found in Bordeaux. There it is used to make fine dry Graves wines. It's also left to sweeten on the vine and be blended into the fabulous dessert wines of Sauternes. It was transported to the Loire River valley during the Dark Ages by the monks of the early Christian Church. In the Loire Valley, Sauvignon Blanc is called Blanc Fumé. In 1966, American wine innovator Robert Mondavi appropriated the name Fumé Blanc for his winery, and many US wineries followed suit. The trend is now reverting toward the use of Sauvignon Blanc on the label by most wineries. In the US, Sauvignon Blanc and Semillion are now successfully being blended by some wineries such as Lyeth and Vichon (*See* Semillon discussion).

Merlot

(Mair-lo) medium bodied to mid-heavy red wine
ORIGIN: France
RECOMMENDED BEST COUNTRIES: France, US, Chile, Yugoslavia and the Balkans
TASTE: Dry (around .25% residual sugar)
COLOR: When a few months old, ruby red to scarlet purple; ages to garnet red quicker than Cabernet Sauvignon.
SMELL (AROMA AND BOUQUET): Rich, pungent, fruity, herbaceous, soft-roasted
HOW TO SERVE: Serve at a cellar temperature of 60°F. Complements beef tenderloin, lamb, venison, turkey, and beef-rich Italian pasta sauces.
PRICE RANGE: $5.00 to $25.00
BEST BUY : $10.00 to $15.00
IMPORTANT ORIGIN FACTS: The Merlot grape is blended with the Cabernet Sauvignon grape to produce the great Red Bordeaux

wines of France. The Merlot grape is used in a larger proportion than the Cabernet Sauvignon grape for the production of Pomerol and St. Emilion wines in Bordeaux. Some wineries in California produce a 100% Merlot, but they also blend it with the Cabernet Sauvignon grape to produce a softer Bordeaux-style wine.

The Merlot grape produces a round, soft, and fruity wine when not blended. In California, the 100% Merlot wines have extraordinary complexity and finesse.

Three round, supple, inexpensive Merlot wines that I tasted recently are the Chateau Souverain and the *M.G. Vallejo* from California and the *Concha Y Toro Merlot Cabernet* from Chili. All were excellent. Three of the finest premium Merlots come from Hogue, Sterling and Clos du Bois. Many of the prestigious California and Washington state wineries are making Merlot. Ask for the youngest vintages available.

Cabernet Sauvignon

(Ka-behr-nay So-veen-yohng) mid to heavy bodied red wine
ORIGIN: France
RECOMMENDED BEST COUNTRIES: US, France, Chile, Italy, Spain, Australia, Yugoslavia, Israel
TASTE: Usually dry (.25% residual sugar to 1% residual sugar)
COLOR: When young, ruby red to purple red; light garnet red when aged.
SMELL (AROMA AND BOUQUET): Rich, earthy, complex, herbaceous, cassis (red current), and raspberries.
HOW TO SERVE: Keep at a cellar temperature of 55°F. Open 30 minutes before tasting to let the smell (bouquet) mix with air so it becomes complex. Complements beef tenderloin, lamb chops, veal, duck, venison, squab, goose. Drink at cool room temperature no higher than 65°F.
PRICE RANGE: $5.00 to $99.00
BEST BUY : $7.00 to $17.00 premium —$18.00 to $65.00 super premium
IMPORTANT ORIGIN FACTS: The grape was originally brought to Bordeaux by the ancient Phonecians from the Caucusus mountains of Armenia. When Julius Caesar arrived in 56 B.C., the Cabernet Sauvignon was being grown widely by the Gaullic tribesmen. He found it made excellent table wine for his legions. The Roman Catholic Church, and later the British people, made this grape known worldwide. Through the marriage of Eleanor of

Aquitaine to Henry Plantagenet in 1152, the British gained control of Bordeaux. They did much to improve the production and quality of the Cabernet Sauvignon grape. They were finally expelled in 1453, but their contributions, along with those of the Romans and Phoenecians, will long be appreciated. The grape is the chief grape of most Red Bordeaux wines and is credited with departing the nobility to these famous wines. Cabernet Sauvignon is also harvested to produce great red wines in the United States that rival their French counterparts.

I have sampled recently two new vintage Cabernet Sauvignon wines that are good in taste and very reasonable in price. Try *Concha Y Toro Chilian* and *M.G. Vallejo California.*

You can establish your own standard of quality for Cabernet Sauvignon wines by tasting either a Beaulieu Vineyard *Rutherford*, Robert Mondavi, Heitz Cellars, or Beringer Cabernet Sauvignon. You will remember their rich tastes and deep bouquets.

CONFUSION: *Cabernet Franc* (Ka-behr-nay Frahng), *Petit Verdot* (Puh-tee Vair-doh), and *Malbec* (Mal-beck) are red grapes blended with Cabernet Sauvignon grapes in France to make the great French Bordeaux red wines. Currently, in California, Cabernet Franc, Petit Verdot, Merlot, Malbec, and Cabernet Sauvignon are being blended into Bordeaux-Style great American red wines. Fine examples are *Opus One, Lyeth Red*, and *Sterling Private Reserve Red Table Wine.*

Chardonnay

(Shar-doh-nay) mid to full-bodied dry white wine.
ORIGIN: France
RECOMMENDED BEST COUNTRIES: US, France, Chile, Spain, Australia, Yugoslavia.
TASTE: Dry, (.25% residual sugar) velvety smooth, buttery, roundness of flavors, richness burst on your taste buds.
COLOR: Pale clear water when very young. When aged, hue resembles golden straw.
SMELL (AROMA AND BOUQUET): Very complex, slight touch of oak, blend of lemon, grapefruit and lime flavors. Sweet yet dry. Delicate yet strong.
HOW TO SERVE: Slightly chilled but not cold. Let it breath by opening 15 minutes before serving; air and Chardonnay mix well to enhance the complex taste and smell (bouquet). Serve with orange

roughy, monk fish, shrimp, catfish, salmon (smoked or grilled), rabbit, sweetbreads, scallops, barbecued chicken, duck or pork shoulder. Chardonnay usually accentuates richer seafood dishes, especially shellfish.

PRICE RANGE: $5.99 to $45.00

BEST BUY : $11.00

IMPORTANT ORIGIN FACTS: The Chardonnay grape variety originated in Burgundy and Champagne districts of France. The Chardonnay grape produces some of the greatest and most complex white wines. All usually age well. The Chardonnay is the most famous of all white grapes and produces the great burgundies of France. In Chablis, France, the Chardonnay is used to make the bone-driest of all white wines. Chardonnay is almost singularly responsible for the "White Wine" explosion in California. Hundreds of wineries there produce a spectrum of distinguished dry wines ranging from heavy, oaky wines dripping with butter to wines of delicate fruit, possessing the finesse of great French Burgundies.

The Chardonnay grape is also indigenous to both the Champagne and Burgundy districts of France. It's used in Burgundy to produce the great estate wines, Le Montrachet, Batard Montrachet, and Chevalier Montrachet. The great Burgundys are very expensive and should only be considered for very special occasions. The Burgundy district of France produces the village wines of great quality like Meursault, Puligny, and Pouilly. The French attach the names of famous estate vineyards to the village names to help sell more wine, (Puligny to Montrachet). The village wines run in price from $12 to $25 a bottle. I suggest the Meursault by Louis Jadot or by Bouchard Pere et Fils. Unlike Cabernet Sauvignon and other red wine grapes, Chardonnay is seldom blended with other white grapes. Its magnificence stands on its own!

The Chardonnay grape is also used to make great Champagnes. Taittinger *Comtes de Champagne Blanc de Blanc* is made from the first pressing of the Chardonnay grape, and made from only Chardonnay grapes. This is an example of a fine vintage champagne.

The word *Cuveé,* when used to describe a Champagne label like Taittinger *Brut La Francaise* non-vintage simply means the bottle is a blend of Champagne reserves. The reserves may also contain blends of Pinot Noir and Chardonnay. Pinot Noir grapes have a red skin, but when crushed the red skin is separated and filtered out, so you have a clear juice made from a red grape. The Chardonnay grape has neutral- to green-colored skin with clear juice inside.

Chardonnay grapes are the principal grapes of the premium California sparkling wine industry. Some sparkling wine houses of California, such as Schramsberg and Domaine Carneros, rival the French Champagnes on the world market.

Three excellent, inexpensive Chardonnay wines are *Napa Ridge* made by Beringer, *Woodbridge* by Robert Mondavi, and *M.G. Vallejo*. Vallejo "Val" Haraszthy, the winemaker for Vallejo, is the great, great grandson of both Agoston Haraszthy and General Mariano Vallejo.

Among the great American Chardonnays are Monticello, Robert Mondavi, Beaulieu, Beringer, Meridian, Mayacamus, Chateau St. Jean, Kendall Jackson, Sequoia Grove, and many others.

Chenin Blanc

(Shay-nan-Blohng) light white wine
ORIGIN: France
RECOMMENDED BEST COUNTRIES: US, Israel, France
TASTE: Dry (.25% residual sugar) to semi-dry (2.5% residual sugar)
COLOR: Water white when first made; pale straw with age
SMELL (AROMA AND BOUQUET): Lemon tart, grapefruit-lime, intense fruity freshness.
HOW TO SERVE: Chilled with "tailgate-picnic lunches", turkey, ham, cheese, tuna and chicken sandwiches, barbecue pork, beef or ribs, cole slaw, potato salad, and baked beans.
PRICE RANGE: $5.99 to $8.99
BEST BUY : $6.99
IMPORTANT ORIGIN FACTS: This grape became popular in America when returning World War I Army Air Force Veterans recommended it. They enjoyed the Vouvray wine from the city of Tours located in the Loire Valley of France. Vouvray is made from Chenin Blanc grapes. Another famous Loire wine, both still and sparkling, that is made from the Chenin Blanc grape, is called *Saumur*. Robert Mondavi and Peter Mondavi marketed the first U.S. Chenin Blanc in 1955 at the Charles Krug Winery in the Napa Valley of California. Many wineries followed the Krug

original, and today we are fortunate to have many excellent dry and crisp examples on the American market.

Chenin Blanc can be a completely dry and delightful wine with great finesse or a semi-dry to sweet, dull wine with very little character. I recommend the crisp Chenin Blancs of both the Grand Cru Winery, located in the Sonoma Valley, and the Beringer Winery situated in the Napa Valley. Robert Mondavi makes a world class Chenin Blanc year after year.

Another of my favorite wines made from the Chenin Blanc grape is *Bouvet Saumur Brut Sparkling*, produced in the Loire Valley of France. It is dry, crisp, and delightful. Bouvet is better than most other sparkling wines that are twice its price.

Chenin Blanc is blended into many generic wines, especially the higher quality white table wines such as vintage Beaulieu (B.V.) Chablis.

Zinfandel

(Zin-fan-dell) medium to heavy-bodied red wine
ORIGIN: Apulia, Italy. Located in the "heel of the boot" of Italy. Some experts, however, consider it to be of unknown origins.
RECOMMENDED BEST COUNTRIES: US
TASTE: Usually dry (.25% residual sugar). Sometimes high alcohol with 2% residual sugar.
COLOR: Purple red when young; garnet red when aged.
SMELL (AROMA AND BOUQUET): Red current and blackberry mix, toasty and warm, earthy, cedary, rich raisin fullness, powerful and fruity.
HOW TO SERVE: Keep at cellar temperature—55°F. Open 40 minutes before tasting. Let air mix with wine in your glass by swirling slightly. The breathing of the wine enhances its flavor. Serve with most Italian dishes like spaghetti, lasagna, manicotti, and ravioli. It also complements beef stew, game, cajun food, hamburgers, peppercorn steak, rack of lamb, and, especially, braised calf liver.
PRICE RANGE: $6.49 to $16.99
BEST BUY : $9.00
IMPORTANT ORIGIN FACTS: The Zinfandel grape was thought to have originated in Hungary. Just recently, American grape growers found it growing in the heel of the boot of Italy—the

Apulia region. The Zinfandel is a clone of the Apulian Sangiovese grape. Many American Zinfandel vines are more than 100 years old—average life is about 18 years. It's usually available in two varieties. One is light and fruity with a pronounced berry flavor; it's similar to Beaujolais in color and it needs a little aging. The other is a rich, dark, full-bodied wine with good tannins; it's made for laying down in the Bordeaux style.

This grape produces superb long-lasting, rich and flavorful red wine. Some of today's Zinfandels are similar in quality and complexity to our best Cabernet Sauvignon. Great "Zin" has a distinct aromatic, raspberry-blackberry fragrance whose intensity increases with wine quality.

I would like to recommend two inexpensive "Zins" that I particularly enjoy. The Heitz Cellars and Beringer wineries produce two of the most charming and typically delightful "Zins" on the market. They are not loaded down with acid, so buy the youngest vintage available. Kenwood *Jack London* is a superb example of a Zinfandel that can be aged in your cellar easily for four or five years. It should be handled like a great wine because it is one.

Pinot Noir

(pee-no N'war) heavy-bodied red wine
ORIGIN: France
RECOMMENDED BEST COUNTRIES: France, US.
TASTE: Dry (around .25% residual sugar)
COLOR: When few months old, purple to ruby red; garnet to orange red when aged.
SMELL (AROMA AND BOUQUET): Rich-earthy, sweet-pungent, robust-ancient, soft yet firm.
HOW TO SERVE: Keep at Cellar temperature—55°F; open 45 minutes before serving to let the wine receive oxygen so that the bouquet will flourish. Serve with game, venison, turkey, prime beef, steaks, lamb, and hamburgers.
PRICE RANGE: $8.99 to $99.00
BEST BUY: $12.00
IMPORTANT ORIGIN FACTS: Pinot Noir grapes were found by the Roman legions of Julius Caesar growing in the Burgundy and Champagne Districts of France. The grapes were probably brought to Marseilles by the ancient Phoenecians and carried northward by Greek colonists living in Provence. The Christian Church, the

Emperor Charlemagne (768-814), and the Duke of Burgundy improved the quality of this "noble and shy bearing grape." It is the only grape allowed by law to be used in the great French Red Burgundies.

The Pinot Noir grape is indigenous to Burgundy and also grows abundantly in the Champagne district of France. Champagne (white sparkling wine) is made from red Pinot Noir whose skins are removed immediately after crushing to prevent the red pigment from infiltrating the grape juice. The flesh inside the red grape produces the clear liquid. As previously discussed, Pinot Noir is often blended with Chardonnay for many cuveés of champagne and sparkling wine, especially from California. Except for champagne or sparkling wines, Pinot Noir is almost never blended with any other grape. In Burgundy, quality value varies greatly depending on the particular shipper or negociant.

Pommard is the name of another prominent village wine made from the Pinot Noir grape. A great monastery wine called *Clos Vougeot*, is also a great burgundy wine. Clos Vougeot Rouge (red) is made from Pinot Noir grapes.

In California, the Pinot Noir grape is used for wines simply called Pinot Noir. Robert Mondavi produces an excellent Pinot Noir Reserve. Beaulieu Vineyard also makes an excellent Carneros Pinot Noir. Great things are predicted from those cooler winegrowing regions of the American Northwest, as well as from the cooler regions of the northern coast of California, such as the Carneros region. Carneros Creek Winery lies on the western slopes of the Mayacamus Mountains in the Sonoma County Carneros Region. Along with Saintsberry, Carneros Creek makes some fine, rich Pinot Noirs.

In the Champagne district of France, Taittinger produces a white Champagne. It is made from a blend of the Pinot Noir and Chardonnay grapes. The Pinot Noir is used in the Burgundy district of France, in the Champagne district of France, and in California.

Schramsberg is one of the very best California sparkling wines. Schramsberg produces a Blanc de Noir sparkling wine from Pinot Noir grapes. Blanc de Noir means "white of black." Remember when you think Pinot Noir, think of Champagne, French Burgundy, and California Pinot Noir (after the grape variety). Famous

Champagne houses include Taittinger, Ayala, Deutz, De Venoge, Moet Chandon, and Bollinger.

Grenache Rosé
(Gren-Nahsh-Ro-Zay)
ORIGIN: France
RECOMMENDED BEST COUNTRIES: US, Israel, France
TASTE: Usually dry (.25% residual sugar) to semi-dry (1.5%)
COLOR: Pale pink when young: orange pink when aged.
SMELL (AROMA AND BOUQUET): Reminiscent of fresh newly pressed grapes and fragrances of newly fermented wine.
HOW TO SERVE: Chill slightly. Do not over chill because serving it too cold will mask its aroma. Serve with ham, chicken, tuna, shrimp, and crabmeat salads. I suggest Grenache Rosé to new wine drinkers because of its sweet and sour taste. It complements most light dishes and is wonderful at tailgate-picnic lunches.
PRICE RANGE: $7.00 to $9.99
BEST BUY : $8.49
IMPORTANT ORIGIN FACTS: This grape is used to make the wonderfully dry and fresh Provence and Tavel Rosé Wines from the south of France. It is also used as a blending grape in *Chateauneuf du Pape* and *Côte du Rhone* wines. Its origin goes back to the Greek and Roman colonists that civilized the ancient Provence region in the south of France.

Wine freshness, even with age, is an attribute of this grape. One of my favorite wines is *Chateau d'Aqueria Tavel Rosé* from the Southern Rhone Valley of France. The Tavel area uses the Grenache grape as one the basic blending grapes for its world famous wines.

We are finding fewer dry Grenache Rosé wines from California. I would suggest that you taste test each one before serving it with your fine dry foods.

Gamay
(Ga'May), light red wine
ORIGIN: France
RECOMMENDED BEST COUNTRIES: France, US
TASTE: Dry to semi-dry
COLOR: Bright ruby when young; dull ruby when aged.
SMELL (AROMA AND BOUQUET): Reminiscent of freshly crushed grapes, delicate sweet aroma.

HOW TO SERVE: Cool 55°-60°F with fish, chicken, turkey, veal, and ham. Goes well with light picnic fare—cold roast beef—and light pasta dishes too!

PRICE RANGE: $5.00 to $15.00

BEST BUY : $7.00 to $10.00

IMPORTANT ORIGIN FACTS: The Gamay grape was brought to France by the Roman legions. It is now planted as a staple crop south of Macon in the southern part of Burgundy. Julienas is a Grand Cru Beaujolais from a village which was named after Julius Caesar. The famous *Côte de Brouilly Grand Cru Beaujolais* is from a hilltop vineyard on Mont Brouilly. The true Gamay grape was transported from the southern Burgundy-Beaujolais district of France to California. Wine labeled just "Beaujolais" is meant to be drunk young—fresh—after 2 to 3 years of vintage. When Beaujolais attaches the word "villages", i.e. "Beaujolais-Villages", it is made in 32 designated villages in Beaujolais, and is of higher quality and should be drunk within 3 to 4 years of vintage. *Nouveau Beaujolais* should be drunk "now." It will not age.

Some of the most velvety-smooth and fruity wines in the world come from the Grand Crus of Beaujolais. Specific village wines include: Julienas, Chenas, Moulin-a-Vent, Morgon, Fleurie (the most delicate), Chiroubles, St. Armour, Brouilly, and Cote de Brouilly. The Grand Crus increased to ten in 1988 with the addition of the very fine and reasonably priced Regnie. Drink these within 2 to 5 years. Morgon may last longer in good vintages. The Grand Crus are the highest quality and will not even have the name "Beaujolais" on the label.

CONFUSION: We don't believe there are many Gamay vineyards in the United States. The Gamay grape from Beaujolais (southern part of Burgundy) and the *Gamay-Beaujolais* grape grown in California are not the same. The Gamay Beaujolais is a derivative of the Pinot Noir grape from the Rhone River valley of France.

Syrah

(See-ra) heavy bodied red wine

ORIGIN: Rhone Valley, France

RECOMMENDED BEST COUNTRIES: US and France

TASTE: Dry (.25% residual sugar)

COLOR: Ruby red when young to garnet red when aged.

SMELL (AROMA AND BOUQUET): Full and pungent, flavorful, slight alcoholic scent, sweet-toasty, and fresh roasted.

HOW TO SERVE: Cellar temperature 60°F. Open 20 minutes before tasting to let the smell (bouquet) mix with air so as to become complex. Complements beef tenderloin, turkey, lamb, venison, pork tenderloin, and beef-rich Italian pasta sauces.
PRICE RANGE: $11.00 to $20.00
BEST QUALITY: $16.00
IMPORTANT ORIGIN FACTS: The original grapevine was brought to the Rhone Valley of France by a returning Knight of the Crusades. According to legend, he first planted it at Hermitage in the Rhone Valley. You find Petite Syrah on some California labels, but this grape is merely a clone, or cousin, of the true Syrah grape.

One of my favorite wines is called *Côtes du Rhone.* It is blended with some Syrah. Look for a reputable shipper. Most of the $2.99 to $3.99 Côtes du Rhone wines "dumped" in some US markets are not advisable. They are thin and watery—not to our liking.

Bouchard Pere Et Fils and *Domaine du Mont-Redon* produce exquisite, thick-bodied, full- flavored, and robust Côtes du Rhone wines. To me, each bottle has sunshine from the beautiful Rhone Valley locked inside. Californians are making more and more true Syrah. It is a "comer." A good one to try is *Meredian* from Pasa Robles.

Other Important Grapes
Familiarize yourself with these, but don't try anything funny.

ITALY
The *Nebbiolo* grape is one of Italy's most important red wine grapes. It produces the famous Barolo and Gattinara wines. They are big, robust red wines from Piedmont in northwestern Italy. Also from Piedmont comes the Cortese grape which produces a great white wine called *Gavi.* It is fresh, dry, and flinty crisp.

The *Brunello* grape from Tuscany produces the famous Brunello Di Montalcino red wine. Dr. Ezio Rivella, Banfi Vintner's wine-maker, is one of Europe's best wine-makers. His Brunello is one of the top quality red wines produced. Nozzole Chianti Riserva is another very famous Tuscan wine. The Sangiovese grape is the main grape for Chianti along with some other blending grapes. Also, we like the reasonably priced and smooth finished Capezzana Chianti.

AUSTRALIA

The Australians produce an excellent Hermitage or *Shiraz* red grape that is soft and smooth to the taste. One of my favorite meals combines Brown Brothers' Australian Shiraz with prime ribs. Most Shiraz wines remind me of the wonderful Merlots produced in California. Shiraz is a clone of the Syrah grape of France. Some micro-climates of Australia produce big, robust, tannic, and long lived Shiraz wines. Your palate is your guide.

SOUTH AFRICA

The *Pinotage* grape from South Africa makes a great red wine. Pinotage is a cross clone of the Syrah and Pinot Noir grapes. The best South African wine that I have ever tasted is an estate bottle Pinotage produced by the farmer Mr. Cozie Stark.

Chapter Seven

Other Types of Wines

My only regret in life is that I did not drink more champagne.
—John Maynard Keynes

Sparkling Wines

Formerly the "drink of the gods," record-breaking quantities of champagne (some of which is actually *not* pink) are now being consumed by rednecks who have discovered that it's not just for New Year's Day anymore. I suggest that you only buy and drink sparkling wines of superior quality. Avoid anything falling into the $2.99 - $3.99 price range. Such "bargains" are almost always made by the *charmat bulk* process. A telltale sign of a charmat product is a plastic stopper instead of a real wooden cork in the bottle. If you see "Charmat" or "bulk process" on the label, avoid that particular brand.

First try a 187ml or 375ml bottle of French, Spanish, or American naturally fermented, *method champenoise* sparkling wine. Some of my favorites are *Taittinger La Francaise, Bouvet Brut French Sparkling, Codorniu Blanc de Blanc Spanish Cava* (Sparkling), *Domaine Carneros Brut, Schramsberg Cremant,* (for a sweeter dessert style), and *Maison Deutz Brut California Sparkling Wine.* Here's our best champagne cocktail recipe (circa 1939): 4 drops of Angostura bitters; 1 tablespoon cognac; 1/4 teaspoon sugar; twist of lime, champagne.

Fortified Wines

Fortified wine is a 10% to 12% wine to which brandy or neutral spirits have been added. A few of the world's fortified wines are Sherry (Spain), Porto (Portugal), Madeira (Island of Madeira), Marsala (Sicily, Italy), and Tokai (Hungary). Fortified wines are usually considered sweet dessert wines, however, a few are bone dry. Some good examples of dry fortified wines are *Harvey's Bristol Dry, Duff Gordon Pinta, Wisdon & Warter Pale Fino Sherry* and *Cossart's Viva Madeira.* The dry fortified wines are excellent with cheese, dried olives, unsalted crackers, as aperitif wines before a meal, or with walnuts and pecans during mid-afternoon. To make sweet fortified wines, the fermentation process is usually stopped. The additional Brandy increases the alcohol strength from 10% to 12% to 18%. The sweetened wine is then aged in oak casks. Perhaps the greatest of these fortified wines are Vintage Ports from Portugal: Taylor Fladgate, Dow's, Graham's, Fonseca, and Harvey. Many great meals finish with a glass of an old famous Vintage Port.

Jug Wines

I advise all my friends to avoid the three and four liter size of jug wines. Buy the 1.5 liter premium varietal wines for your large parties. Some fine California examples are *Robert Mondavi Woodbridge Cabernet Sauvignon, Chardonnay,* and *Sauvignon Blanc; Beaulieu Vineyard Estate Burgundy* and *Estate Chablis; M.G. Vallejo Cabernet Sauvignon* and *Chardonnay; Napa Ridge Chardonnay; C.K. Mondavi Chardonnay and Cabernet.*

Chapter Eight

Wine: A Medicinal Cornucopia

Drink a glass of wine after your soup and you steal a ruble from the doctor.

—Old Russian Proverb

Only a fool doesn't change his mind about wine.

—Victor L. Robilio, Sr.

There is a prevalent puritanical concept in America that if one enjoys something, then naturally that something must be unhealthy. From a very young age, we are warned against the inherent evils of alcohol. Not so; wine is beneficial to both the body and the spirit. Here is where rednecks can benefit most. After years of cornbread, grits, fried chicken, pork, chicken-fried steak, etc. isn't it time you ingested something that made sense?

Recent medical studies, which were the focus of an historic Morley Safer report on "60 Minutes," indicate that red wine actively combats cholesterol. The skin of red grapes are kept in the fermenting process and the chemical, resveratrol (which the grape produces to ward off fungus), serves to decrease cholesterol levels in the human body. Red wine significantly lowers LDL cholesterol levels (the evil component of cholesterol) while raising the levels of HDL (the good guy in the cholesterol scenario). Red Bordeaux wines from France are the strongest cholesterol-fighters because the French grape skins need more resveratrol to ward off the prevalent fungus caused by a marginal climate.

There is more good news. Studies have shown that wine lowers the risk of heart attacks by flushing out the circulatory system, sticky platelets near the heart in particular. A very recent study even proves that wine may help prevent the formation of the gene that causes cancer. The compound quercetin, which is found in red wine, inhibits the cancer gene from converting normal cells to cancer cells.

Wine is rich in iron and in the B class of vitamins. It stimulates the appetite, a property which many older people may appreciate. It aids in digestion by relaxing the stomach, which facilitates the work of the digestive juices. Dry wine is the recommended variety for digestive aid. Wine can even prevent constipation.

Perhaps wine's greatest medicinal asset is its power of relaxation. Wine is absorbed into the bloodstream at a slower rate than hard alcohol so the body is not so shocked by a significant jolt to the pulse rate. The easy way which wine slides into the bloodstream is analogous to wine's ability to restore one's delicate emotional balance, which the pressures of life often disturb.

Wine rednecks should remember that Thomas Jefferson lived to the old age of 83 after a life spent imbibing wine. The next time a friend tries to offer a shot of 100 proof Kentucky Bourbon, the wine redneck, in a very polite yet authoritative tone, should reveal to his friend that a glass of Red Bordeaux would be a much healthier choice.

Wine can be an integral part of a comprehensive health plan, and it's more fun than 800 leg lifts, per leg. However, should the wine redneck do 1600 leg lifts a day, it is highly advisable to do them gently, so that the wine will not spill as the leg is lifted. If the wine redneck is also a calorie counter, then wine is the alcoholic beverage of choice. It has a relatively low calorie count, averaging 96 calories per four ounce glass.

Calories/Nutrition

It is very easy to figure out the number of calories per glass of wine. Just double the alcohol content on the label and you will know the calories per ounce. For example: Robert Mondavi *Cabernet Sauvignon* has 12% alcohol: 12% x 2 = 24 calories per ounce; so a four ounce glass has 96 calories.

Spirits usually give you the proof per gallon. The proof is equivalent to the number of calories per ounce since proof is already double the alcohol content. Should you be drinking a sweet spirit or liqueur, please add a few more calories to your final calorie count per glass.

Chapter Nine

Southern Wineries

No nation is drunken where wine is cheap, and none sober where the
dearness of wine substitutes ardent spirits as the common beverage.
Wine brightens the life and thinking of anyone.
— *Thomas Jefferson*

Although being a redneck is a state of mind, it is nonetheless a
fact that most HONEST TO GOD rednecks live in the SOUTH.
Fortunately, for these on-the-spot wine snobs there are many
excellent Southern wineries. Below is a comprehensive list that
proves one need not travel to the West Coast to experience a
winery.

Alabama

Dora

Braswell's Winery is noted for its native farm table wines, and this
intriguing winery offers a taste of the wines actually produced and
enjoyed in the Old South. Small and unique, the winery makes
sixteen varieties from native Alabama fruits. In addition to the
expected muscadine, scuppernong and grape varieties, Braswell's
also produces elderberry, pear, persimmon, blueberry, blackberry,
and peach wines. Wine and beer-making supplies are also sold on
the premises. From Highway 78 West, turn right onto the
Warrior-Jasper Road, then right onto the Bankhead Highway. Or
call 205-648-8335 for information.

New Market

Alistair Vineyards, 2978 Hurricane Road, New Market, AL 35761,
is only 15 minutes from Huntsville. From U.S. 231, take
Winchester Road 8.1 miles to County Lake Road. Turn right. Go
2.9 miles to Hurricane Road. Turn left and go 1 mile to the
winery. The proprietors, Donald and Noel McCalister, may be

reached at 205-379-3527. The winery is open from May to December from 10 am to 6 pm. The winery is a small, family run establishment which, in addition to excellent wines, also offers incredible Alabama scenery in what is known as "Hurricane Valley." The tasting room, a seventy year old farm house shaded by old sugar maples, has been remodeled; the quaint atmosphere of the tasting room definitely serves to enhance the total experience.

Arkansas

Altus

Post Familie Vineyards and Winery has been run by the same family for five generations, and its tasting room is an experience in itself, finished in redwood from old wine casks. Tina Post says, "Our muscadine wines and grape juices are a favorite among our southern customers, with the fairly new varietal vignoles making a big splash." Open year round (Monday through Saturday, 8 am to 7 pm; Sundays from 12 to 5 pm) the winery offers guided tastings, with wine and cheese alternated to cleanse the palate. The extensive giftshop stocks Arkansas basketry and gourmet food items also. Write them at Rt. 1, Box 1 Altus, Arkansas, 73821, or call 501-468-2741.

Wiederkehr Wine Cellars, Altus, Franklin County, Arkansas. Should you be driving from Little Rock, Arkansas to Fort Smith on Interstate 40, do stop at Wiederkehr Wine Cellars. They have a nice casual restaurant plus tastings and tours of the winery and vineyards which are geographically located on top of St. Mary's Ozark Mountain. Their restaurant and winery telephone number is 501-468-2611. We suggest you stay at the Best Western Motel located in Clarksville, Arkansas and drive the twenty minutes to Wiederkehr. They produce a wide range of wines and champagnes. Wiederkehr's tour hours are Monday through Saturday 8:30 am till 4:30 pm. After 4:30 pm tours are by appointment only. Their address is Route 1, Box 14, Altus, AR 72821, or call 501-468-WINE.

Florida

Alva

Eden Vineyards Winery and Park is the southernmost winery in the U.S.A., only 15 minutes from Fort Myers. Run by the Kiser family, it is the sole source of *Tropical Carambola*, made from "star fruit," first produced in 1990 by vintner Mary Studt, formerly of Inglenook. Eden offers a highly stylized list of light, dry elegant wines, without sacrificing quality to its strong regional identity. Its *Lake Emerald* is featured at the Grand Floridian Hotel of Disneyworld. You'll also want to try its *Alva White, Alva Rouge, Coral Bell* (a sweet blush, with a very crisp finish) and *Edelweiss*, another Studt creation. Eden also produces a very popular dessert wine, *Eden Spice*, with a velvety texture. The winery is open from 11 am to 5 pm seven days a week, excluding major holidays. There is an annual hiatus from August 19 to September 8, but all other times, you can have a tour from 11:30 am to 3:30 pm. Phone the winery at 813-728-9463, or write (19850 State Road 80; Alva, FL 33920).

Clermont

Lakeridge Winery and Vineyards (19239 U.S. 27 North; Clermont, Florida; 34711) is noted for sparkling and table wines made from Muscadine and Florida Hybrid Bunch grapes. The tasting room features many Florida wines, plus local arts and crafts. Winery hours are Monday through Saturday from 10 am to 6 pm, and Sundays from noon until 6 pm. Closed Thanksgiving, Christmas, and New Year's Day. The owners recommend local restaurants Happ's Crown (1340 E. Highway 50 in Clermont; phone 904-394-3887), and Jack Benny's Barbecue (Highway 27, Minneola; phone: 904-394-2673).

Mississippi

Indianola

Claiborne Vineyards (P.O. Box 350, Indianola, MS 38751) can be reached by driving on Highway 49 West a quarter of a mile north of the Intersection of Highway 49 West and Highway 82.

Claiborne and Marian Barnwell are the owners. Call 601-887-2327 for a tour appoint-ment. Claiborne and Marian produce a variety of wines: *Seyval Blanc, Villard Blanc Vidal Blanc, Bayou Rouge, Baco Noir* (red) *Marechal Foch* (red), Chardonnay and Cabernet Sauvignon. The Comfort Inn on Highway 82 is a pleasant place to stay.

Natchez

Old South Winery, 65 Concord Avenue, Natchez MS 39120. Call Dr. Scott O. Galbreath, Jr. at 1-601-445-9924. The Old South Winery is open until 6 pm daily. He makes a delightful selection of excellent Muscadine wines. Our favorites were: *Miss Scarlet, Sweet Magnolia, Southern Belle* and *Carlos Dry. The Noble,* a red varietal, contains more "Resveratol" than Bordeaux. Resveratol, a natural compound found in muscadines, fights fungal disease and lowers human cholesterol levels. Dr. Scott Galbreath has a farm near Natchez, where his family raises most of his muscadines. You can reach Jackson, Mississippi in about three and 1/2 hours from Memphis. I suggest a famous bed and breakfast, The Millsaps Buie House, located at 628 N. State St., Jackson, Mississippi 39202 (Telephone 601-352-0221). Special attention, care and professional courtesies from the staff will bring you back again and again. Enjoy Jackson, then the next morning drive to Natchez by taking I-55 South and exit at Hazelhurst, then on to Natchez. I suggest the Guest House, a bed and breakfast located at 201 N. Pearl St., Natchez, Mississippi 39120. The warm and friendly Southern hospitality of Louis and Gina Jones will make your stay very restful. It is located within easy walking to the downtown historic areas.

Tennessee

Blountville

Countryside Vineyards and Winery, 1 mile from Exit 63 off I-81, is located at 658 Henry Harr Rd., Blountville, TN 37617 (Telephone 615-323-1660. The winery may be reached from Exit 63 off I-81 by heading north, following this road past the large water tower on the hill and turning right onto Lynn Rd. Within a few hundred yards, turn left onto Henry Harr Rd. and the winery is one-half mile on the left.

Clarksville

Beachaven Vineyards and Winery is a mere 45 minutes from downtown Nashville. The street address is 1100 Dunlop Lane; Clarksville, Tennessee; 37040 (Telephone 615-645-8867). Take Exit 4 off I-24; turn right onto Highway 79. Within a few hundred feet, turn right onto Alfred Thun Road and go two miles until you reach Dunlop Lane. Turn right and you will be there. Summer hours are 10:00 am to 6:00 pm, Monday through Saturday; Sunday noon to 6:00 pm. In winter the winery is open Tuesday through Saturday, 10:00 am to 5:00 pm; Sunday noon to 5:00 pm. They produce a variety of wines, most notably *Beachaven Blush*. Most wines are made from grapes grown in middle Tennessee.

Crossville

Stonehaus Winery, Inc. is located at Exit 320, Genesis Road at Interstate 40, Crossville, TN. It is open from 10 am till 6 pm, Monday through Saturday; 1 pm till 5 pm on Sundays. Reduced winter hours. They produce a wide variety of wines from the Chardonnay to the sweet Muscadine, as well as reds and blushes. Educational tours are offered hourly. Stroll through the Gift Shop and sample homemade fudge and see the wide variety of gifts. Then sample cheese in the Cheese Pantry where they have over 40 domestic and imported cheeses, freshly baked bread and other gourmet items. Their mailing address is Stonehaus Winery, INC., Rt. 2, Box 47H, Crossville, Tennessee; 38555. For information call 615-484-WINE.

Jamestown

The Highland Manor Winery is located on Highway 127 South. For information write Oscar Irving Martin, P.O. Box 213, Jamestown, Tennessee; 38556. Hours are Monday through Saturday, 10 am to 5 pm. He has extended hours in the spring and summer. For more information please call 615-879-9519. You will find a wide variety of wine produced, when available, including Muscadine, Alwood, Catawba, Chardonnay, Concord, Niagara and White Riesling. We suggest The Beggars Castle Restaurant which features German cuisine. Additional points of interest in the vicinity of Highland Manor are The Historic British Colony at Rugby and the Sgt. Alvin York State Historic Site at Pall Mall.

Memphis

Cordova Cellars, 9050 Macon Rd., Cordova, TN 38018. When you visit Memphis, TN., try to stay at The Wilson Inn on U.S. Highway 64 and 40. It is the closest motel to Cordova Cellars. Contact Mary or Randy Birks, 901-754-3442. Tasting and tour hours are Tuesday through Sunday—1 pm to 5 pm. Enjoy the beautiful rolling vineyard land and the clean, well-run wine facility. Tell the Birks that we recommended their Southern wine hospitality! Jim's East Restaurant (901-388-7200) has an excellent menu with casual dining not too far from Cordova Cellars.

Laurel Hill Vineyard, 1370 Madison Avenue, Memphis, TN 38104. Try to stay at the Peabody Hotel, 149 Union Ave., telephone 901-529-4000, which is about 10 minutes away from Ray Skinner's Laurel Hill Winery. For further information call 901-725-9128. Located in a commanding stone building near the corner of Madison Avenue and Cleveland Street, his hours are 10 am to 12:30 pm and 1:30 pm to 5:30 pm Monday through Friday, except November and December when hours are 10 am till 2 pm on Saturday. Ray's vineyards are at Henryville, Lawrence County, Tennessee. He produces a nice variety of dinner wines. We suggest Justine's Restaurant, 901-527-3815, for elegant, Southern antebellum dining—not too far by car from Laurel Hill Vineyard Winery. Marena's, a more causal restaurant, is also nearby at 1545 Overton Park Avenue, 901-278-9774. Other nearby restaurants are The Claybrook at 220 S. Claybrook, 901-725-7585, and Giovanni's at 282 N. Cleveland, 901-725-6660.

Monteagle

Monteagle Wine Cellars is located high above The Cumberland Plateau on top of Monteagle Mountain. Their address is Highway 64-41A (P.O. Box 638), Monteagle, TN; 37356. For information call 615-924-2120. The winery is easy to reach, only 300 yards off Interstate 24 on US 24 on US Highway 64-41A in Monteagle. Take exit 134, turn left at the interchange, drive 300 yards. Tasting room and Retail Sales hours are: April through October—7 am until dark, Monday through Saturday, Sunday noon until 5 pm; November through March—7 am until 5 pm, Sunday noon until 5 pm. They produce an extensive variety of dinner and dessert wines.

Texas

Bryan

Messina Hof Wine Cellars and Vineyards, (4545 Old Reliance Rd., Bryan, TX 77802) has an impressive list of awards, including Best Regional Wine in America. They recently broke ground to double the size of the production area. Owner-winemaker Paul V. Bonarrigo offers an intriguing selection, including the lovely *Angel Late Harvest Johannisberg Riesling,* a delicate dessert wine. He recommends combining his wines with his wine food products, such as his *Traditions Blush* wine with his Jalapeno Blush jelly to serve with ham. Other food products include white Zinfandel marmalade, Chardonnay mustard, and Cabernet Sauvignon jam. Call 409-778-9463 for a calendar of upcoming events or information on daily guided tours and tastings.

Fort Worth

La Buena Vida Vineyards (8917 W. Jacksboro Highway; Fort Worth, Texas; 76135 offers tours by appointment only. Call 817-237-WINE to make your appointment to try its champagne, port, and mead. The tasting room and giftshop are open Monday through Saturday from 11 am to 5 pm, and Sundays from noon until 5 pm. Other area attractions include the Fort Worth Nature Center, and Trinity Meadows Horse Racing Track. The owners recommend two local restaurants: The Wild Onion (817-677-2509) and Vance Godbey's (817-237-2218).

Fredericksburg

The Pedernales Vineyard is five miles south of Fredericksburg on the Kerrville Highway, and is open Mondays through Saturdays from 9 am to 5 pm. Owners Karl and Judy Koch recommend a self-guided walking tour to inspect the source of their very dry Sauvignon Blanc and Cabernet Sauvignon, as well as local wildlife. The winery also has a hand-made mesquite tasting bar, and a historically valuable leaded glass window—enigmatically named the John Dillinger window. Fredericksburg itself is a history buff's dream, and well worth an overnight stay. Local accommodations include the

Peachtree Inn, the Comfort Inn, and the Sundayhouse Inn. The winery's address is HC 12 Box 70 AA, Fredericksburg, Texas; 78624. Telephone: 512-997-8326.

Lubbock

Pheasant Ridge Winery, Route 3, Box 191; Lubbock, Texas; 79401. Open the second Saturday of each month from 10 am to 4 pm, this winery can also be toured by scheduling an appointment for an individual tour. Call 806-746-6750 to make an appoinment. Owner Bobby Cox takes pride in his winery's high percentage of oak cask storage, which produces highly acclaimed Cabernets. The winery also produces Chardonnays and Cox's personal favorite--a very dry Chenin Blanc. After making your selections at the winery, you might try the wonderful country French cuisine at the Frenchman Inn, 4409 19th Street, in Lubbock (806-799-7596). Nearby attractions include the Ranching Heritage Center in Lubbock, and Palo Duro Canyon to the north.

Llano Estacado Winery is the powerhouse of Texas wineries, and, some say, of the South. In less than twenty years since its first commercial planting, Llano (pronounced YAH-no) has grown from being the teaching tool of a Texas Tech professor of organic chemistry to a major winery attracting the attention of national critics with its excellent Chardonnay, considered its "star" wine. But it also produces consistently good Reislings, Gewurztraminers, Chenin Blancs, and Sauvignon Blancs, and well as its "signature" blends. Guided personal tours are available Monday through Saturday from 10 am to 4 pm, and Sundays from noon until 4 pm. The winery is not open on Christmas, New Year's Day, or Thanksgiving Day. Llano is well-equipped for visitors; call 806-745-2258 for details, or write Mary Louise Fuchs at the winery address, P.O. Box 3487; Lubbock, Texas; 79452.

Orange

Piney Woods Country Wines in Orange, Texas is easily accessible from U.S. I-10. When traveling west, take exit 875, and then turn right at the winery sign. When traveling east, take exit 876, turn left at the bayou, and then take the first right. The winery is open 8:30 am till 5:30 pm Mondays through Saturdays; 12:30 pm till 5:30 pm Sundays. Tours for four or more adults are available anytime by appointment. Tours for less than four adults are available by appointment on Saturdays and Sundays. The winery has a tasting room where you can sample up to ten of their wines. Generally, three muscadine wines—one red, one semi-dry white, and one semi-sweet blush—and six to eight fruit wines are available. All of the fruit, which includes strawberry, peach, plum, and pear, is grown in Texas so availability of wine is seasonal. Alfred J. Flies, owner and operator, extends an invitation to stop and taste year round, but he suggests calling ahead if traveling a great distance, as he may be away at tastings and/or meetings. There are five motels within ten miles of the winery and several good restaurants. Write Piney Woods Country Wines at 3408 Willow Drive, Orange, Texas 77630, or call (409) 883-5408.

Austin

Slaughter Leftwich Vineyards is on 50 acres in a stone facility built in the tradition of the early Texas architecture. The winery is noted for its Chardonnay and *Austin Blush*, which are both international award winners. It is located seventeen miles from downtown Austin and can be visited year round for sales and tastings. Take 620 to one mile south of Mansfield Dam and turn onto Eck Lane at the intersection of Hudson Bend Road and 620. Tasting room, which overlooks Lake Travis and the Texas Hill Country, is open Mondays through Saturdays from 1 pm till 5 pm. Tours are available Fridays, Saturdays, and Sundays October-May. From June to September, every day except Monday. Their gift shop offers an extensive selection of t-shirts, sweatshirts, wine jellies, wooden gift boxes, logo wine glasses and cork pullers. The winery owners suggest the Lake Way Inn, which is very near the winery and the Oasis Restaurant, at 6550 Comanche Trail. For more information, write Slaughter Leftwich Vineyards, 4209 Eck Lane, Austin, TX 78734, or call (512) 266-3331.

Virginia

Afton

The vines at **Afton Mountain Vineyards** are among the oldest in Virginia, and owners Tom and Shinko Corpora give credit to this and the "blessed" local climate for their excellent Chardonnay, Cabernet Sauvignon, White Zinfandel, Gewurztraminer, Reisling and Semillon. They expect to produce Pinot Noir and Chenin Blanc in the near future. The winery is open for tours, tastings, and picnics Tuesdays through Sundays from 10 am to 6 pm (5 pm in winter).   Minutes off the Blue Ridge Parkway, this is possibly one of the most scenic wineries in the U.S.A, with a shaded picnic area overlooking the Rockfish Valley and the Ragged Mountains. Local accommodations include bed and breakfasts, such as the Acorn Inn, as well as motels and campgrounds. Charlottesville is only 25 minutes away, and the owners also recommend that while you are in the area, visit Tastings, a restaurant, wine bar, and wine shop in Charlottesville (502 E. Market Street; phone 804-293-3663). Phone the winery at 703-456-8667.

Barboursville

Burnley Vineyards (Rt. 1, Box 122; Barboursville, Virginia; 22923, Telephone 703-832-2828) is near Jefferson's Monticello and Madison's Montpelier. This winery has a tasting room, a small gift shop, and a picnic area. Sample its Chardonnay and Cabernet Sauvignon, as well as its Riesling, Rivanna Sunset, and Somerset. You may wish to stay at Burnley Vineyards guest house in the woods overlooking the vineyards, or the nearby Sleepy Hollow Bed and Breakfast. For dinner, the owners recommend The Toliver House in nearby Gordonsville (703-832-3485).

Esmont

Open to the public from 10 am to 4 pm, the **Chermont Winery** produces a Riesling, Chardonnay, Cabernet Sauvignon, and a blush. The tasting room has a home-like atmosphere. Nearby attractions include Monticello, Ash Lawn, the University of Virginia, and the James River. For bed and breakfast, try High Meadows, Chester Bed and Breakfast, or Chermont Bed and Breakfast. Shop for pewter in Chermont, and check out Lumpkins Restaurant in nearby Scottsville. For more details, write the Chermont Winery at Rt. 1, Box 59; Esmont, Virginia, 22987, or phone 804-286-2211.

Lovingston

La Abra Farm and Winery is noted for its sweet peach wine, and its *Harvest Red* and *Skyline Red*, which are blends. La Abra offers tours daily from 1 pm to 5 pm, except in January, February, and March, when they close on Mondays and Tuesdays. Located "in Thomas Jefferson's backyard," La Abra is close to many historic attractions. Lovington's Village Inn is the recommended local hotel (804-263-5068) and for dining, you might try McGritz on Rt 29 near Lovingston (804-263-8388).

Meadows of Dan

The **Chateau Morrisette Winery** boasts a beautiful wood and stone tasting room, where you must be sure to sample the Sweet Mountain Laurel, Merlot, and Vidal Blanc, among other notable varieties, before enjoying your favorite choice with a meal at the restaurant on the premises. Nearby history includes Mabry Mill, and the Blue Ridge Parkway, as well as a plethora of antique shops. For overnight stays, the owners recommend the Woodberry Inn, The Oaks, or the Doe Run Lodge. For more information, write the winery at P.O. Box 766; Meadows of Dan, Virginia, 24120.

Oak Grove

Ingleside Plantation Vineyards is located in historic Westmoreland County, 2.5 miles south of Oak Grove on Rt. 638. This winery is open year round except major holidays, and the hours are 10 am to 5 pm, Mondays through Saturdays; noon to 5 pm on Sundays. Tour the winery to taste its award-winning Cabernet Sauvignon, Chardonnay, and champagne. You'll also want to see its permanent exhibits, including colonial wine implements, Chesapeake waterfowl carvings, and American Indian artifacts. Carl Flemer planted the first Ingleside grapes in 1960; twenty years later a French-trained oenologist, Jaques Recht, was sailing the Potomac and decided to join Flemer permanently. This winery is well worth a visit, and Washington's birthplace, Robert E. Lee's home Stratford Hall, and historic Fredericksburg are all nearby. For excellent dining and overnight accommodations, try The Inn at Montross (804-493-9097). Write the winery at P.O. Box 1038; Oak Grove, Virginia; 22443, or call 804-224-8687.

Painter

Combine the pleasures of Virginia's Eastern Shore (Chincoteague or Assateague and other barrier islands) with a visit to **Accomack Vineyards**, 17030 Coal Kiln Road; Painter, Virginia; 23420. This small winery is noted for is Cabernet Sauvignon and Merlot. Tour and tasting hours are 10 am to 4 pm Mondays through Saturdays; 1-5 pm Sundays. Closed on Thanksgiving, Christmas and

New Year's Day. The giftshop offers many varieties of wines, as well as other items made on the Eastern Shore. There are many hotels and motels in the area to choose from, and the winery recommends that you dine at the Captain's Deck in Nassawadox, and Beachway in Chincoteague.

Williamsburg

The **Williamsburg Winery, Ltd.** has the specially designed appearance of 17th and 18th century wine-making operations, but it houses state-of-the-art equipment and produces a notable list of offerings. James River White is a light dinner wine, and Governor's White is a semi-fruity blend of Riesling and Vidal; you'll want to be sure to sample both. Tours are available Tuesday through Sunday from 10 am to 5 pm except from January 15 through February 15. A $3.00 fee includes a guided tour and a tasting of 5-6 wines served with crackers and cheese. The gift shop stocks hundreds of wine-related items, including T-shirts. The winery address is P. O. Box 3592; Williamsburg, Virginia; 23187. There is no restaurant on the premises of the winery, but the owners recommend The Trellis (804-229-8610), located on Duke of Gloucester Street in Williamsburg. In addition to the phenomenon of Williamsburg itself, you'll want to see Busch Gardens, Water Country U.S.A., and the Kingsmill Resort while in the area.

Victor L. Robilio Jr.

Author, connoisseur, wine merchant and
friend of Rednecks.